ISRAEL

FOR CRITICAL THINKERS

CUFI PRIMER

RICHARD BASS

Editor: Jamie Bush
Cover/book Design: Tibor Choleva
Photo Research: Melissa McClellan
Proofreader: Sara Davies

Photo Credits:
Creative Commons: François-Joseph Navez (p 9); David Germain-Robin (p 12); Jewish Agency for Israel (p 15); Jewish Agency for Israel (p 28 bottom); Government Press Office (p 30); p 32 (top); Ilan Bruner (p 32 bottom); Library of Congress: American Colony Jerusalem Collection (p 13 top);
Map Illustrations (all): Joshua Avramson
Public Domain: Heinrich Bünting (p 4); Valentin de Boulogne (p 10); Myrabella (p 11); John Collier (p 16); p 19; p 20; Edward N. Jackson (US Army Signal Corps) (p 23); Rudi Weissenstein (p 26); p 27; Kluger Zoltan (p 28 top); p 28 (top inset); CIA (p 34, p 35); David Falconer (p 35 inset); B. Železník (p 38 top); Paul Morse (p 38 bottom); Shutterstock.com: © Boris-B (p 5 left); © kavram (p 5 right top); © Rostislav Glinsky (p 5 right bottom); © AridOcean (p 6); © Creativemarc (p 7 left top); © Noam Armonn (p 7 right top); © maxmacs (p 7 middle right, left); © Michal Ninger (p 7 right bottom); © kavram (p 7 left bottom); © Karol Kozlowski (p 14); © Ryan Rodrick Beiler (p 36); © Rostislav Glinsky (p 39, p 40)

Printed in China

CHRISTIANS UNITED FOR ISRAEL

THE BETTER WE UNDERSTAND ISRAEL, THE BETTER WE CAN STAND WITH ISRAEL.

On behalf of the leadership of Christians United for Israel, I want to thank you for your generous gift which enables us to further our mission to stand with the Jewish State. I am eternally grateful to you for investing your time to learn the truth about Israel's embattled history, her tireless quest for peace, and why and how Christians should support Zion at this critical time in history.

We live in a world where evil shrouds itself in the fog of political correctness as well as the catchwords of a social gospel. We daily witness those of either malicious intent or self-imposed ignorance make every effort to delegitimize and demonize Israel and the Jewish people. This narrative to vilify Israel has sadly crept into our government, our college and university campuses and even within the walls of our churches—but it cannot stand up to reality. Evil is the enemy of good and a lie is the enemy of truth and because of God's infallible Word we stand on the side of truth concerning Israel and the Jewish people.

This insightful book will inform and inspire you. It is filled with intriguing facts about Israel that you will want to share with family, friends, and others. It is our prayer that as you use it to better understand Israel, that it will likewise equip you to better stand with Israel.

Thank you for being part of the CUFI family who has come together in unity from all parts of the world with our pledge—"For Zion's sake I will not hold My peace, And for Jerusalem's sake I will not rest . . ." (Isaiah 62:1).

May the Lord bless you with good health, abundant joy and supernatural favor as you help bless Israel and the Jewish people.

John Hagee

Pastor John Hagee
National Chair
Christians United For Israel

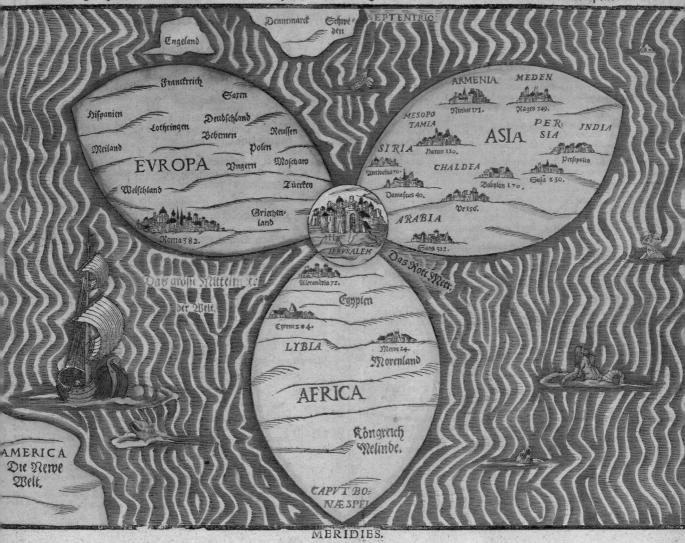

The Bünting Map, published in 1581, is a historic illustration of the world. The three continents of the Old World are shown divided by the seas, but connected by Jerusalem — the hub of the world because of its religious importance.

It is a land that has gone by various names. English ones include Israel, Canaan, the Promised Land, the Holy Land, Judea and Samaria, and Palestine. The first of these names—Israel—is derived from the name given to the biblical Patriarch Jacob, whose descendants became the Israelites. The last one, Palestine, is derived from the name of one of its ancient occupants: the Philistines. This was the name the Romans gave to the land around the second century CE to replace the name Judea, and it was taken up by the post-Roman empires of Europe and Islam. We will refer to this land as Israel.

This land's importance in human history is out of all proportion to its size. Many millennia ago, Israel saw the dawn of human civilization, and it has since played a central role in the story of humanity. It is sacred to the three great monotheistic religions of the world, Judaism, Christianity, and Islam. Collectively, these religions are followed by more than half the peoples on earth.

The Abrahamic religions, Judaism, Christianity, and Islam, consider Jerusalem a holy city. Each of these religions has sacred sites there. (Clockwise from left: Church of Holy Sepulchre, Western Wall, and Dome of the Rock.)

Israel's story is an ancient one. In the West (and especially in North America), 250 years is considered a long time. It is longer, for example, than the United States of America has existed as a nation. The history of human civilization in Israel, by comparison, dates back many thousands of years. The actors in this ancient story include the most powerful world empires of the past—the Egyptians, Assyrians, Babylonians, Persians, Greeks, Romans, and Ottomans. The most recent chapter concerns the modern State of Israel.

Today, Israel is a land coveted by two peoples, Arabs and Jews. The conflict between their national aspirations, ongoing now for almost a century, has caused much hardship on both sides. Each side subscribes to versions of the past that support their respective territorial claims. We can't hope to understand the problems in this region without knowing the actual history.

Some people refer only to recent and current events when explaining the problems now facing the Middle East. A more complete understanding of what's happening today must start thousands of years ago, when the land was called Canaan.

A COMPLETE UNDERSTANDING OF WHAT'S HAPPENING TODAY MUST START THOUSANDS OF YEARS AGO, WHEN THE LAND WAS CALLED CANAAN.

BEFORE THE ISRAELITE CONQUEST: 1800–1250 BCE

CANAAN IN THE SECOND MILLENNIUM BCE

The physical position and the topography of Israel have profoundly shaped its history. In the ancient world, Canaan was a point of intersection between different peoples and worlds. Its geographical position made it a natural corridor between Asia and Africa. To the west, the Mediterranean opened to the civilizations of the Aegean world. Nomadic tribes of the Arabian desert populated the region's eastern edge. Canaan was a major transit area and junction for trade. Caravans crisscrossed the country carrying goods between the Nile Valley and the Euphrates, as well as to Arabia and the busy Mediterranean seaports of Phoenicia.

The topography within Canaan promoted variety in its inhabitants, and its population was not a single nation but an ethnic patchwork of peoples. The terrain was unusually diverse for such a small area. From west to east, the land changes dramatically. The Mediterranean basin gives way to a mountain ridge in the centre of the country, which in turn drops steeply to the Jordan rift valley. In the north lie the Golan Heights, and in the south is the Negev desert. This division of Canaan into hills and valleys and varied ecosystems naturally produced diversity in the peoples living there. Before the Israelite conquest, Canaan was a land of heterogeneous city-states that were, quite often, fighting amongst themselves.

The lack of political or cultural unity within Canaan left the territory particularly vulnerable to the major powers of the time. Egypt lay to the south, and to the north were the Hittite Empire and the various nations of

Canaan's geographical position made it a natural corridor between Asia and Africa. The area of Canaan, as described in the Bible, roughly corresponds to modern-day Lebanon, Israel, Gaza, The West Bank, the western part of Jordan, and southwestern Syria.

Mesopotamia and beyond. Why would these superpowers be interested in this tiny strip of land?

Dominance over Canaan brought great political advantages. Militarily speaking, its geographical location made ancient Canaan strategically important as a bridgehead. Control of it was needed for any attack by one power upon another. That is why this land became an international battleground more often than any other area in the ancient world. From the dawn of human history, then, Canaan was exposed to and periodically dominated by the earliest centers of civilization, which provided a continual stream of settlers into the region. Through the millennia, as we noted above, the ethnic make-up of Canaan became extremely mixed. Before the Israelite conquest and settlement of the land c. 1250-1200 BCE, various peoples, of assorted ethnic and cultural backgrounds, inhabited the land. The ones mentioned in biblical sources include Amalekites, Hittites, Jebusites, and Amorites, as well as Canaanites (Numbers 13:29). Egyptian documentary sources, such as the El Amarna letters, attest to this biblical picture of diversity.

THE PATRIARCHAL PERIOD

The proto-history of Israel, spanning the generations from Abraham to Jacob in the Bible, is known as the Patriarchal period. What we know about it is based partly on the biblical account, partly on the findings of modern scholarship. Extra-biblical sources, documentary and archaeological, tell us that the Bible stories are consistent with demographic and historical conditions of the time.

The Patriarchal period is very relevant to our understanding of current events. The covenantal promises described in the biblical account are crucial to the territorial claims of the peoples now in conflict over Israel. In some cases, the adherents of Judaism, Christianity, and Islam interpret these promises differently.

The varied ecosystems of the Canaan region naturally produced diversity in the many peoples living there.

THE BIBLE AS HISTORY?

Many are not used to approaching the Bible as work of history. Is it really a credible source of factual information? Aren't its narratives just myths and folklore that have been passed down for thousands of years?

The prevailing views about this question have shifted back and forth in the last two centuries. Until about 1800, most people took the biblical stories to be literally true. They accepted the Bible as a reliable account of ancient history. This changed in the 19th century, when German textual scholars began to argue that the early biblical narratives were largely myth, no more factual than Greek stories of Hercules. This skeptical view of the Bible prevailed into the first decades of the 20th century. It is still the view of many.

Over the past hundred years, there has been a shift away from this purely skeptical view and a restoring of credit to the biblical account. This change is owing to modern science; it has radically revised our understanding of antiquity. Archaeologists of the last half century, instead of dismissing ancient texts and their stories out of hand, have used them to guide their excavations. In the light of recent decades' discoveries, some of the biblical stories have taken on a fresh historical reality.

This is not to say that everything in the biblical account has been scientifically proven. The more remote in time the people and events being described, the less scientific evidence there is to support their historical authenticity. In the Bible's earliest books, especially, we cannot always find archaeological evidence to substantiate what's written. Where these books are concerned, modern investigators have uncovered circumstantial evidence for some of the events described—places and names, migratory patterns, and customs. But there isn't much evidence concerning specific people and events.

This changes once we get to the later books. The events they describe, including the stories of the ancient Israelite kingdoms, date from around 2,800 years ago. With these books, there is strong direct evidence that the events in the narrative occurred. For example, the written records of other empires—the Egyptians, Babylonians, and Assyrians—support the biblical account. The Bible is not a history book. But it contains a great deal of information about ancient history and culture, and some of this information is supported by modern archaeological and documentary evidence.

Whether or not one accepts the Bible, the fact remains that the story of Abraham and his descendants is integral to three of the world's great monotheistic religions—Judaism, Christianity, and Islam. As such, this story has altered the course of history and affected millions of people over several millennia. And if our aim is to gain some understaning about how and why Israel is significant to Jews, Christians, and Muslims, we need to understand the biblical narrative.

A SKEPTICAL VIEW OF THE BIBLE PREVAILED INTO THE FIRST DECADES OF THE 20TH CENTURY. IT IS STILL THE VIEW OF MANY.

THE BIBLICAL NARRATIVE

The first patriarch described in the Bible is Abraham. According to the biblical account, Abraham received a divine directive to go from his home in Haran (northwestern Mesopotamia) to the land of Canaan—that is, present day Israel. There, according to scripture, God made a covenant with Abraham. He promised to give the land to Abraham and his descendants, and in return the Israelites were to worship God alone and to obey his laws. The notion that God gave the Land of Canaan to the Israelites is a basic tenet of Judaism. In Judaism, the nation (or people), the Bible, and the land are all connected.

When Abraham received this promise, he had no heirs. The Bible tells us that he was 85 years old, and his wife Sarah 75. Sarah assumed she was too old to bear children. Following the custom of the time, she offered her handmaiden Hagar to Abraham, so that Abraham could produce an heir. Hagar gave birth to a son named Ishmael.

Shortly afterwards, Sarah herself gave birth to a son named Isaac. As the boys grew older, Sarah became concerned about inheritance rights and demanded that Abraham send Hagar and Ishmael away. According to the biblical account, Isaac was Abraham's rightful heir, and the land of Canaan was his legacy. Isaac is the second biblical patriarch.

In the biblical narrative, Isaac's son Jacob becomes the third biblical patriarch. Jacob is renamed Yisrael (Israel) after his struggle with a divine being. This is the source of the name Israel. Jacob's twelve sons were called B'nei Yisrael, which literally means "the Children of Israel." In the Bible, the descendants of Jacob's twelve sons become the ancient Israelites.

ABRAHAM IN JUDAISM, CHRISTIANITY, AND ISLAM

Jews, Christians, and Muslims alike accept Abraham as a prophet and consider Ishmael and Isaac to be the patriarchs of the Arab and Jewish people, respectively. The casting-out of Hagar and Ishmael is the point in the story where the Judeo-Christian narrative diverges from the Islamic one. According to Islamic tradition, Abraham did not cast Ishmael out. Rather, God ordered him to take Hagar and Ishmael to Mecca, where Abraham later returned, with Ishmael, to build the Ka'aba—the most sacred shrine of Islam. Muslims turn in its direction when praying.

The biblical account of the patriarchal period stands as as a remarkably complete and detailed record, unique for its time, of an ancient people's coming into being. One eminent scholar of Jewish history has observed that

> of no people in the biblical period other than Israel has there been preserved such a detailed account of its proto history or, certainly, such a complete and continuous description as is to be found in the patriarchal narrative and in the Exodus-Conquest cycle.

A depiction of Hagar and Ishmael in the desert by François-Joseph Navez. Ishmael is recognized by Muslims as the ancestor of several prominent Arab tribes and as the forefather of Muhammad.

9

RISE OF CHRISTIANITY IN ISRAEL: 1ST CENTURY CE

Jesus is Christianity's central figure. According to Christian theology, the events of his life took place in the 1st century CE, during the time of the Roman occupation of Israel. Jesus is believed to have been born around the dawn of the Common Era in Bethlehem, just south of Jerusalem. The facts of his early life are uncertain, but there is general agreement that he was a Jew who was familiar with the Torah and the Law of Moses. In his spiritual teaching, he incorporated Torah precepts, the most fundamental of which is monotheism. The Christian New Testament, particularly the Gospels, recounts the major events of Jesus's life. These took place in the Galilee, in northern Israel (Samaria), and in Judea. According to Christian scripture, Jerusalem and the surrounding area were the site of the Last Supper and of Jesus's arrest, trial, Crucifixion, burial, and resurrection.

After Jesus's death, it was Paul, a Jewish convert to the new religion who never physically met Jesus, who carried the message of Christianity to Rome and to various parts of the Roman Empire. Paul was active around the middle of the first century of the Common Era. Largely through his efforts and influence, Christianity underwent tremendous growth in the first and second centuries.

By the year 64, some two years after the death of Paul, Christianity had become widespread in Rome. But the Roman emperors of the time, Nero and Domitian, saw the new religion as a political threat and outlawed it. The course of Christianity could have ended there. Instead, something remarkable happened in 312 that led to Christianity's being established as the official state religion of the Roman Empire.

Paul is generally considered one of the most important of Jesus's apostles. Today, his epistles continue to be vital roots of the theology, worship, and pastoral life in the Roman and Protestant traditions of the West, as well as the Orthodox traditions of the East.

What happened was the conversion to Christianity of Constantine I. He was the emperor of Rome from 306 to 337. The motives behind Constantine's conversion were likely political and pragmatic rather than spiritual. Nonetheless, his conversion contributed greatly to the spread of the faith and helped transform the Roman province of Palaestina into a Christian Holy Land.

In 326, Constantine's mother Helena, a fervent Christian, visited Jerusalem. During her visit, she tried to locate Christianity's sacred sites—for example, the sites of Jesus's crucifixion and burial. As a result of her findings new structures were eventually built in Jerusalem, the most important being the Church of the Holy Sepulchre. According to Christian theology, this is where Jesus was crucified, where he was buried, and where he was resurrected. The name of the Holy City was also changed from Aelia Capitolina—the name the Romans had given it after the second Jewish rebellion, in 135 CE—back to Jerusalem.

Christianity dominated in Israel until the 7th century CE, when Islam rose to power and took control of the region.

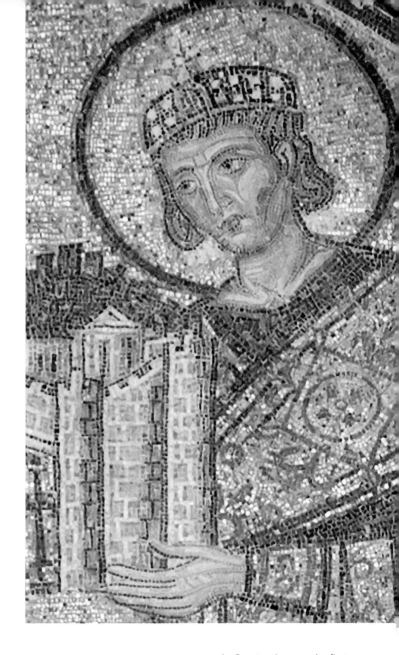

Constantine—as the first Christian emperor—is a significant figure in the history of Christianity. The Church of the Holy Sepulchre, built on his orders at the purported site of Jesus's tomb in Jerusalem, became the holiest place in Christendom.

AFTER JESUS'S DEATH, IT WAS PAUL, A JEWISH CONVERT TO THE NEW RELIGION, WHO CARRIED THE MESSAGE OF CHRISTIANITY TO ROME AND TO VARIOUS PARTS OF THE ROMAN EMPIRE.

THE LATIN KINGDOM: 1099–1291

Toward the end of the 11th century, Europeans launched the first of many Christian Crusades to take the Holy Land back from the Muslims. They were successful in 1099. Their victory led to the establishment of the Latin Kingdom in Israel. Archaeological evidence of Latin Crusader presence has been found on many sites in Israel.

At its height, in the mid-12th century, this Christian kingdom roughly encompassed the territory of modern-day Israel and the southern parts of Lebanon. The Crusaders massacred both Jews and Muslims in the course of their conquest.

THE CRUSADERS MASSACRED BOTH JEWS AND MUSLIMS IN THE COURSE OF THEIR CONQUEST.

Belfort Castle was a Crusader fortress located in Southern Lebanon. Saladin captured it in 1190.

THE OTTOMAN EMPIRE IN ISRAEL: 1517–1917

At the beginning of the 16th century, the Ottoman Empire conquered the Levant and in the process took Israel from the Mamelukes. The Ottoman Turks, the last of the great Islamic empires, had sovereignty in the area until they were defeated by the Allied Powers in World War I.

After the war, the Allied Powers gave to the Arab people the Ottoman Empire's former territories, today called Saudi Arabia, Syria, Lebanon, Jordan, and Iraq. During the same period, they granted Israel to the Jewish people. It is these two peoples, the Arab and the Jewish peoples, that are in conflict today in Israel.

The Ottoman surrender of Jerusalem to the British forces took place on December 9th, 1917.

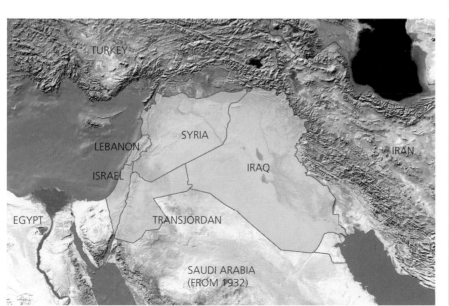

Ottoman territories given to Arabs and Jews after WWI, showing modern borders.

JEWISH AND ARAB NATIONALISM

The term *Zionism* is derived from the word *Zion*, a frequent synonym in the Bible for "Jerusalem."

The Jewish and Arab nationalist movements emerged more or less simultaneously toward the end of the 19th century, an era of many nationalist movements. Both peoples sought land in the Middle East to achieve their goals, and both turned to the European powers for help. In 1920, in San Remo, a small town on the Italian Riviera, the Allied Powers, with the support of the 51 member states of the League of Nations, set in motion the events that would bring both peoples, Arab and Jews, the right to govern themselves. The lands allocated for the Arab peoples encompassed most of the Middle East. The Jews were to have a small strip of land on the Mediterranean coast. This section will focus on how these movements and decisions came to pass.

POLITICAL ZIONISM

The term *Zionism* is derived from the word *Zion*, a frequent synonym in the Bible for "Jerusalem." Numerous verses in the Bible refer to "Zion" or "Mount Zion" and directly associate Zion with Jerusalem, a city central to Judaism for millennia and mentioned in the Bible over 600 times.

In the 19th century, a Jewish nationalistic movement arose whose aim was to re-establish Jewish sovereignty in Israel after nearly 2,000 years. The term *Zionism*, first used in the 19th century, has come to refer primarily to this political and nationalistic aspiration.

ZIONISM AND RELIGIOUS ZIONISM

The desire to return to Zion—to Jerusalem and the land of Israel—has been expressed in daily Jewish prayers since the days of the Babylonian exile 2500 years ago. A longing for Jerusalem and for the Land of Israel is part of Judaism. Judaism does not separate its world view from its concept of nationhood and of a homeland. In Judaism, the Bible, the nation (or people), and the land are all connected. The Land of Israel, then, has always been sacred to religious Jews, a land they believe was promised to them by God and to which they are bound to return with the coming of the Messiah, as foretold in biblical prophecy.

Many religious Jews rejected political Zionism when the movement began. They did so on the grounds that it was a secular, socialist (i.e., atheistic) movement and that an attempt to recover the Land of Israel by human—rather than divine—agency was blasphemous.

Religious Zionists sought to reconcile religious Jews to political Zionism. Led by their chief spokesman, Rabbi Abraham Isaac Kook (1865–1935), they aimed to provide religious legitimation for the political movement. Their justification was as follows: political Zionism, though conceived and led by secular Jews, was not merely a secular phenomenon; it was the tool by which God promoted his scheme of returning world-wide Jewry to the Land of Israel, where they were to establish a sovereign Jewish state in which Jews would live according to the laws of Torah.

Some religious Jews have never been reconciled to political Zionism or to the existence of the State of Israel.

Abraham Isaac Kook was the first Ashkenazi Chief Rabbi of the British Mandatory Palestine. Rav Kook built and maintained channels of communication between the various Jewish sectors, including the secular Jewish Zionist leadership, the Religious Zionists, and non-Zionist Orthodox Jews.

POLITICAL AND LEGAL FOUNDATIONS OF ISRAEL

WORLD WAR I: PLEDGES AND AGREEMENTS

World War 1 changed the course of history for both the Arab and the Jewish peoples. It ultimately created the Middle East we see today. By the time the war broke out, the Arab and Jewish nationalist movements were seeking territory to fulfill their aims. The Jews sought Israel, and the Arabs sought an area that included the Arabian Peninsula, Mesopotamia

Lieutenant Colonel Sir Arthur Henry McMahon was a British diplomat and Indian Army officer who served as the High Commissioner in Egypt from 1915 to 1917.

(Iraq), and Syria, as well as Israel. All of these lands had belonged to the Ottoman Empire for approximately five centuries. They would likely have remained so had it not been for the Great War.

On October 31st, 1914, the Ottoman Empire joined the Central Powers (Germany and the Austro-Hungarian Empire) in the war against the Allied Powers (the British Empire, France, Russia, and their various secondary allies). The Turkish decision increased the significance of the Arab people to the Allies. Why?

The Allied Powers feared that Turkey, the premier Islamic state, would rouse the Arab Muslim world and its tens of millions against them. If Turkey announced that it was at war with the Christian powers of Europe and that the Islamic holy places were in danger, Muslim Arab believers would rally around the banner of the faith.

To prevent this from happening, the Allied Powers looked to ally themselves with the Arabs against the Turks. Their aim in doing so was not only to boost their war effort but to protect their economic interests in the region. This was especially the case for Great Britain, which had vital interests in the Middle East, including the Suez Canal and valuable oil-fields at the head of the Persian Gulf.

The Arab nationalists, for their part, saw that an alliance with the Allied Powers could help them throw off the Turkish yoke and further their goals of Arab independence. Arab nationalists approached the Sharif of Mecca, Husain Ibn Ali—the leading figure in the Arab-Islamic world—with a proposal. They told Husain that they favoured a revolt against Turkey, and they asked him whether he would lead the independence effort. There ensued meetings between Husain's youngest son, Faisal—who was acting as his father's deputy—and six principal Arab leaders. They presented Faisal with a plan of action as well as the terms under which they would agree to cooperate with Great Britain against Turkey. Their plan was to have Husain approach the British with their proposal. Husain agreed to do so, and the Arab leaders pledged to recognize him as the spokesman of the Arab race.

Husain then sent a letter to the British. He told them that he would lead an Arab revolt against the Ottoman Empire in return for an understanding with the British as regards territory. This produced a famous series of letters that have come to be called the McMahon–Husain correspondence.

BRITISH PLEDGES TO THE ARAB PEOPLE

In the course of the McMahon–Husain correspondence, the British pledged territory to the Arab people. During the same period—as we shall see—the British were pledging territory to the

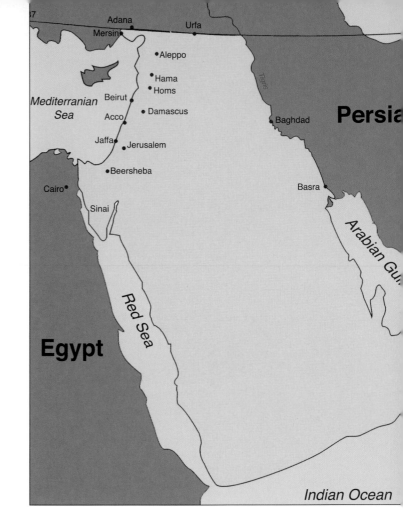

Jewish people. These different pledges came into conflict in the area then called Palestine.

Husain's initial letter to McMahon stated the terms on which the Arab leader was prepared to enter an alliance with Great Britain. Husain demanded that Great Britain recognize the independence of the Arabs in all the territory from the Persian frontier (today's Iran) in the east to the Mediterranean Sea in the west; and from today's northern borders of Syria and Lebanon to the southern tip of the Arabian Peninsula.

In other words, the land Husain requested included the current countries

Map of Husain's territorial demands reflecting his vision of a United Arab kingdom.

▨ Territory requested by Sharif Husain

WAS PALESTINE PLEDGED TO THE ARABS?

The Arabs concluded from the McMahon–Husain correspondence that all of Palestine, including Jerusalem and its Old City, was pledged to them. The British have always denied that this was their intention.

In support of their denial, the British cite the "modification" included in McMahon's response to Husain. McMahon explicitly excluded certain regions from his territorial pledges to Husain. His wording was as follows:

> The districts of Mersin and Alexandretta, and portions of Syria lying to the West of the districts of Damascus, Homs, Hama, and Aleppo, cannot be said to be purely Arab, and must on that account be excepted from the proposed delimitation.

Twenty-five years later, the British government published a report on the controversy over the McMahon–Husain correspondence. Their aim was to adjudicate between the Arab and the British interpretations. Arab representatives as well as British ones were included in the enquiry.

The Arabs concluded the following: "Such geographical description as he [McMahon] and the Sharif give of the portions to be reserved points unmistakably to the coastal regions of northern Syria."

The British representatives, for their part, claimed that McMahon's response to Husain "excluded, and should reasonably have been understood to exclude, the part of southern Syria, consisting of portions of the former Vilayet of Beirut and the former independent Sanjaq of Jerusalem, now known as Palestine." The British also quoted McMahon's views on the matter: "I feel it my duty to state, and I do so definitely and emphatically, that it was not intended by me in giving the pledge to King Husain to include Palestine in the area in which Arab independence was promised."

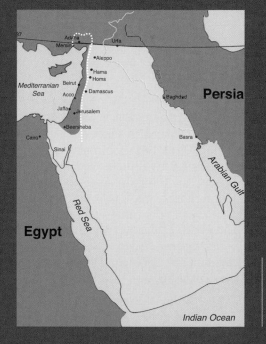

Map of McMahon's Delimitation of the proposed Arab Kingdom.

• • • • • Western limit to Arab Kingdom proposed by McMahon

of Israel, Lebanon, Syria, Jordan, Iraq, and Saudi Arabia. He wanted this whole region to become one unified Arab State.

McMahon responded. He said that Great Britain was prepared to recognize and uphold Arab independence in all the territory proposed except for portions of land on the Mediterranean coast. He was referring to the region comprising what is now Lebanon and Israel. His wording was indefinite, however. The territories covered in the British pledge were not clearly defined, and this later resulted in much controversy.

British Pledges to the Jewish People

As McMahon and the Sharif of Mecca were exchanging letters, the British government was meeting with representatives of the Jewish people and discussing territorial pledges with them. In 1917, Weizmann, now the president of the Zionist Organization, submitted a proposal to the British government regarding Palestine. The famous declaration that was based on Weizmann's proposal and finally issued by the British government became known as the Balfour Declaration.

The particular wording of the Balfour Declaration was problematic in the long run. It used the phrase "national home," which, unlike the word "state," was unknown in international usage and had no established legitimacy.

THE TERRITORIES COVERED IN THE BRITISH PLEDGE WERE NOT CLEARLY DEFINED, AND THIS LATER RESULTED IN MUCH CONTROVERSY.

THE BALFOUR DECLARATION

His Majesty's Government view with favour the establishment in Palestine of a national home for the Jewish people, and will use their best endeavours to facilitate the achievement of this object, it being clearly understood that nothing shall be done which may prejudice the civil and religious rights of existing non-Jewish communities in Palestine, or the rights and political status enjoyed by Jews in any other country.

The Balfour Declaration (dated November 2nd 1917) was a letter from the British government's foreign secretary Arthur James Balfour to Baron Rothschild, a leader of the British Jewish community. The text of the letter was published in the press one week later, on November 9th 1917.

THE SAN REMO CONFERENCE

The next round of meetings concerning the former Ottoman territories took place in 1920, in the Italian resort city of San Remo. The Allied Powers convened there to establish the map of the "new" Middle East. Significant decisions were made. From the San Remo meetings emerged Mandates for Syria, Mesopotamia, and Palestine.

GREAT BRITAIN'S MAIN RESPONSIBILITY
IN PALESTINE WAS TO FOLLOW THROUGH
ON THE BALFOUR DECLARATION'S PLEDGES
REGARDING THE NATIONAL HOME FOR THE
JEWISH PEOPLE.

San Remo is very important in regards to Israel. It established that the Balfour Declaration would be incorporated into the Mandate for Palestine. By incorporating the Declaration, the Mandate for Palestine became a special case, fundamentally different from the Mandates for Syria/Lebanon and Mesopotamia. Understanding this difference is a key to understanding the Zionist claim to Israel.

The Mandates for Syria/Lebanon and Mesopotamia were focused on the actual communities living in those regions: the current inhabitants. In other words, the Mandatories of these regions were bound to consider—to accept as a "sacred trust"—the rights, interests, and wishes of the Arab populations currently living there.

World leaders in front of Villa Devachan in San Remo, Italy, where the conference took place. The San Remo conference established that the Balfour Declaration would be incorporated into the Mandate for Palestine.

The Mandate for Palestine, based on the Balfour Declaration, would not do this. In Palestine, the Mandatory (Great Britain) would not be responsible for assisting the predominant population (that is, the Arabs) to achieve self-determination. Instead, Great Britain's main responsibility in Palestine was to follow through on the Balfour Declaration's pledges regarding the national home for the Jewish people.

In other words, the San Remo Resolution fused two important ideas: the pledge of the 1917 Balfour Declaration, and the principles of Article 22 of the Covenant of the League of Nations. In doing so, it accomplished three things. First, it officially identified Palestine as the place where a Jewish national home would be established. Second, it reserved this Jewish national home not just for the 60,000 Jews living in Palestine at the end of World War I, but for the Jewish people as a whole—that is, for the approximately 15 million Jewish people worldwide. Palestine, as a leading British statesman said at San Remo, "was in the future to be the National Home of the Jews throughout the world." Third, it made the Jewish people worldwide the beneficiary of the principle of self-determination: one of the principles of Article 22 was that the developing nations being helped by the Mandatories were entitled to future self-government and independence. In the case of Palestine, this entitlement went not to the current Arab majority but to the existing and prospective Jewish inhabitants.

KEY PROVISIONS OF THE MANDATE FOR PALESTINE

Preamble: Whereas the Principal Allied Powers have agreed that the Mandatory should be responsible for putting into effect the declaration [the Balfour Declaration] originally made on November 2nd, 1917, by the Government of His Britannic Majesty, and adopted by the said Powers, in favor of the establishment in Palestine of a national home for the Jewish people, it being clearly understood that nothing should be done which might prejudice the civil and religious rights of existing non-Jewish communities in Palestine, or the rights and political status enjoyed by Jews in any other country; recognition has thereby been given to the historical connection of the Jewish people with Palestine and to the grounds for reconstituting their national home in that country; and

Article II: The Mandatory shall be responsible for placing the country under such political, administrative and economic conditions as will secure the establishment of the Jewish national home, as laid down in the preamble, and the development of self-governing institutions, and also for safeguarding the civil and religious rights of all the inhabitants of Palestine, irrespective of race and religion. ...

Article IV: An appropriate Jewish agency shall be recognised as a public body for the purpose of advising and co-operating with the Administration of Palestine in such economic, social and other matters as may affect the establishment of the Jewish national home and the interests of the Jewish population in Palestine, and, subject always to the control of the Administration to assist and take part in the development of the country.

Article V: The Mandatory shall be responsible for seeing that no Palestine territory shall be ceded or leased to, or in any way placed under the control of the Government of any foreign Power.

Article VI: The Administration of Palestine, while ensuring that the rights and position of other sections of the population are not prejudiced, shall facilitate Jewish immigration under suitable conditions and shall encourage, in co-operation with the Jewish agency referred to in Article 4, close settlement by Jews on the land, including State lands and waste lands not required for public purposes. In Article IV, recognition was given to the Jewish right to "large-scale" immigration into Palestine.

Articles IV and V contained provisions protecting the rights of the Arab tenant farmers and keeping Muslim Holy Places under the custody of Muslims.

The Mandate document provided that Arabs living in Palestine would receive civil and religious rights, but not sovereignty rights. This was in keeping with Faisal's formal ceding of Palestine to Weizmann and the Zionists prior to and during the Paris Peace Conference. But the San Remo decisions also benefited the Arab people tremendously in terms of their territorial goals. The Allied Powers created mandates for Syria and Mesopotamia (Iraq)—that is, for most of the Middle East. With these mandates in place, tens of millions of Arabs received sovereignty rights in those regions, ending 500 years of Turkish rule. The San Remo decisions were ratified by the 51 members of the League of Nations in 1922, making them binding in international law.

THE MANDATE FOR PALESTINE, ARTICLE 22, AND THE PRINCIPLE OF SELF-DETERMINATION

When it came to the Mandate for Palestine, the Allied Powers chose to make the Jewish people worldwide, not the Arabs in Palestine, the beneficiaries of the "sacred trust" described in Article 22. This meant that the right to self-determination in Palestine went to the Jewish people, not to the Arab majority there.

The Arabs believe this decision was unjust. Their reasoning is simple: at the beginning of the 20th century, they themselves were the majority population in the region and had been since the 13th century CE. Their view is that Wilson's principle of self-determination should have applied to them, and they should not have been disposed of—"dominated and governed"—except by their own consent.

The Jewish people point to other considerations. They point to the fact that Palestine was their ancient homeland and that Palestine had been Turkish territory, not Arab territory, since 1517. The Supreme Council of the Allied Powers and the 51 member states of League of Nations gave to the Arab peoples all of the Turks' former territory in the Middle East except for the very small portion reserved for the Jewish people. A commission headed by Woodrow Wilson—who introduced the concept of self-determination and was himself fully in favour of a Jewish state in Palestine—explained as follows the Allied Powers' support for the Zionist plan:

It was the cradle and home of their vital race, which has made large spiritual contributions to mankind, and is the only land in which they can hope to find a home of their own, they being in this last respect, unique among significant peoples.

When Faisal appeared before the Supreme Council on February 6th, he specifically excluded Palestine from the territory he asked for. This exclusion was consistent with the Faisal–Weizmann Agreement he had made only weeks before.

Palestine was always a special case within the mandate system— a prospective state not for the Arab majority living there in 1919, who at the time numbered approximately 600,000, but for the Jewish people throughout the world, who numbered 15 million. By the unique terms of the Mandate for Palestine, in other words, the Jewish people were the majority population in Palestine and warranted the right to self-determination.

Woodrow Wilson of the United States (right) was fully in favour of a Jewish state in Palestine. He and (left to right) David Lloyd George of Britain, Vittorio Orlando of Italy, and Georges Clemenceau of France formed the Council of Four—the top Allied leaders who met at the Paris Peace Conference.

THE UNITED NATIONS AND THE PARTITION OF PALESTINE

The UN General Assembly received the UNSCOP recommendations and approved Resolution 181 (the "Partition Resolution") on November 29, 1947. Thirty-three nations voted in favor of it. Since Resolution 181 was a General Assembly motion (rather than a Security Council decision), it was not binding in international law; it could become a legal agreement only if both Jewish and Arab representatives accepted it.

The Jewish leadership had compelling reasons to reject the Partition Resolution. From their point of view, it would have meant the second time in 30 years that Palestine had been partitioned to the significant territorial advantage of the Palestinian Arabs. The national home for the Jewish people under the British Mandate, as set out at San Remo, was to include territory on both the east and west sides of the Jordan River. If we take into account the previous partition of Palestine—the one that, in 1921, created Transjordan in the territory east of the Jordan river—this new plan meant that the Jewish state was to be established in a territory approximately one-eighth the size of the territory originally allotted for it.

But the Jewish leadership accepted the resolution. Pressure on them to do so came from several sources. Not the least consideration was the fact that hundreds of thousands of European Jews, displaced by World War II, were living in refugee camps with nowhere to go.

Table showing Arab and Jewish demographics under the Partition Plan.

Territory Allocation	Arab and Other Population	% Arab and Other	Jewish Population	% Jewish	Total Population
Arab State	725,000	99%	10,000	1%	735,000
Jewish State	407,000	45%	498,000	55%	905,000
International*	105,000	51%	100,000	49%	205,000
Total	1,237,000	67%	608,000	33%	1,845,000

Source: UNSCOP Report 1947

*The U.N. plan called for an expansion of the municipal boundaries of Jerusalem to create an Arab majority in the International Zone.

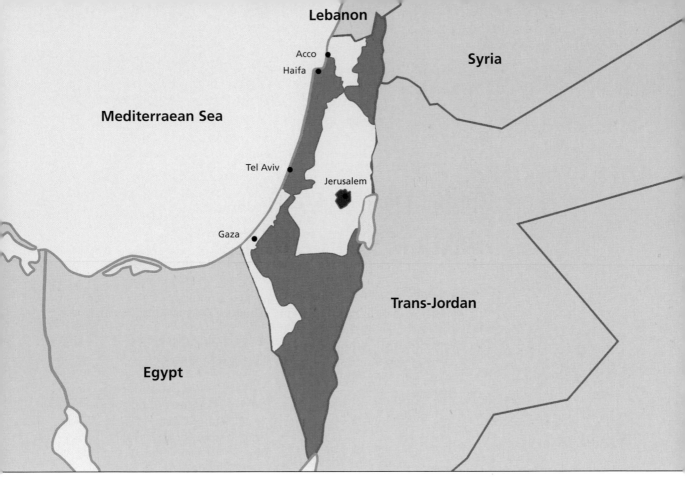

Map of United Nations Partition Plan for Palestine, adopted on November 29th 1947.

- Proposed Arab State
- Proposed Jewish State
- Jerusalem (International Zone)

Jewish reservations about the new partition plan proved irrelevant. The Arab leadership flatly rejected it. And they made it clear that any attempt to implement it would lead to war. Why did the Arab leaders reject the 1947 partition plan? They thought it unfair that it gave 57 percent of the land to 37 percent of the people. Their view was that the Jews ought to be a minority population in a unitary Palestinian state.

Did the Arabs have a point? After all, the Jews constituted only about 30 percent of Palestine's population in 1947. Arab objections need to be considered in the context of all of the regional mandates and their allocations. The Mandates for Syria and Iraq gave political rights to the tens of millions of Arab people living in the remaining regions of the Middle East—millions of square miles of land that, until that point and for hundreds of years previously, had been sovereign Turkish territory.

By contrast, the Allied Powers reserved an area of approximately ten thousand square miles for the 15 million Jewish people around the world who would be prospective citizens of the Jewish state.

THE JEWISH LEADERSHIP ACCEPTED THE RESOLUTION. THE ARAB LEADERSHIP FLATLY REJECTED IT. AND THEY MADE IT CLEAR THAT ANY ATTEMPT TO IMPLEMENT IT WOULD LEAD TO WAR.

THE 1948 WAR
AND ITS LEGACIES

The British completed the withdrawal of their armed forces on May 14, 1948, and Israel declared independence the same day. The next day, Arab armies from Transjordan, Syria, Lebanon, Iraq, and Egypt attacked Israel.

The Arab League explained the invasion to the UN as a necessity, a means of establishing security and order. The UN rejected this rationale for military force.

The war continued through 1948 and into the next year. In early 1949, after UN-mediated discussions, Israel signed an armistice agreement with Jordan.

TERRITORIAL EFFECTS: THE WEST BANK

The 1949 Armistice Line—the Green Line—has become one of the most significant dividing lines in Middle East history. It demarcates the territory now called the West Bank, so named because it's on the west bank of the Jordan River. Prior to the 1948 war, there was no distinct territory called the West Bank. The territory took on that name only after Jordan occupied it in the wake of the 1948 War. Before that, it was called Judea

Territory held on June 1, 1948 after the initial Arab Invasion.

Territory held by Arabs

Territory held by Israel

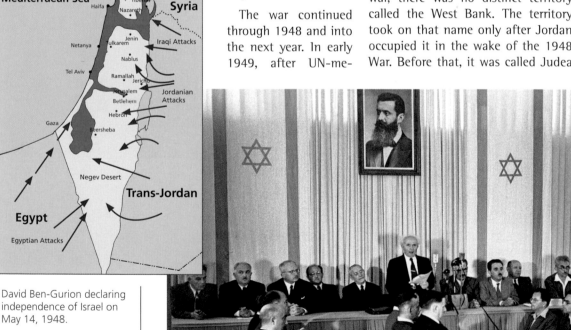

David Ben-Gurion declaring independence of Israel on May 14, 1948.

and Samaria and was considered part of the national home for the Jewish people under the Palestine Mandate.

According to the provisions of the 1949 Armistice Agreement, the Green Line did not constitute a border and was not supposed to be used to determine territorial rights. Nonetheless, the UN continually evokes it in its efforts to broker peace between Israel and the Palestinian Authority. Almost every Arab–Israeli peace plan has earmarked the West Bank as the territory of the future Palestinian state.

Israeli policemen meet a Jordanian legionnaire near the Mandelbaum Gate on the Green Line that divided Jerusalem between 1949 and 1967.

REFUGEES

Another legacy of the 1948 war was refugees. As a result of the war, hundreds of thousands of Arabs who lived west of the Jordan River were displaced. The Palestine Arabs referred to their displacement as the *Nakba*—the catastrophe. The Palestinian Authority hold Israel responsible. They are supported in this by the UN and by many members of the international community. Some have alleged that Israel engaged in the "ethnic cleansing" of Judea and Samaria (the West Bank) during the war. Supporters of the Palestinian Authority maintain, further, that Israel should allow the refugees from the 1948 war to return to their original homes or should compensate them and their descendants for the loss of their property and livelihoods.

The 1948 Armistice Agreement and the Green Line.

    Territory held by Arabs

    Territory held by Israel

━━━   Green Line

LOCATION OF THE HOLY SITES

If the Green Line were to become the border between Israel and a future Palestinian state, the following holy sites would no longer be located within the State of Israel: the Temple Mount in the Old City, which is Judaism's holiest site and the ultimate bone of contention in the Arab–Israeli conflict; and the Church of the Holy Sepulchre, which covers the ground on which Jesus was crucified and buried.

Does it matter who controls these Jewish and Christian holy sites? History shows that the religious rights and holy sites of all faiths in the Old City have fared best under Israeli control. Between 1948 and 1967, when the Jordanians governed the Old City, synagogues were destroyed, cemeteries desecrated, and Jews prohibited from entering the Old City or from worshipping at the Western Wall. Jews were not given access to the sacred Jewish burial grounds on the Mount of Olives. The Jordanians also prevented Christians from visiting their holy places except for special ceremonial events, such as Christmas. This contravened the 1949 Armistice Agreement. Since 1967, the freedom of worship and the holy sites of all faiths have been respected.

JEWISH REFUGEES

The caption for the main image:

A Yemenite family walking through the desert to a camp near the seaport city of Aden in Yemen. 49,000 Yemenite Jews were airlifted (inset) to safety in the new state of Israel between June 1949 and September 1950 during an operation called Operation Magic Carpet.

The 1948 war also created a Jewish refugee problem. After the war, Jewish people living in Arab countries suffered a backlash. This happened in Iraq, for example, where Jewish communities had existed for 2,500 years. (They had been there since the first diaspora, which followed the Babylonian conquest of Judea.) Hundreds of Jews in that country were murdered, thousands imprisoned, and Jewish synagogues, shops, and homes were burned and destroyed. This pattern was repeated in other Arab countries. Between 1948 and the mid-70s, over 800,000 Jews were stripped of all they owned and driven out.

Jewish refugees at Ma'abarot transit camp. The Ma'abarot were refugee absorption camps in Israel in the 1950s. The camps were meant to provide accommodation for the large influx of Jewish refugees and new Jewish immigrants arriving in the newly independent State of Israel.

The UN has passed a number of resolutions concerning the rights of Arab refugees and runs an entire organization specifically for Palestine Arabs called UNWRA. But no UN resolutions have been passed concerning Jewish refugees—the civilian populations expelled from Arab countries. (In November 2013, the government of Canada published a report titled "Recognizing Jewish Refugees from the Middle East and North Africa").

The majority of Jewish refugees were absorbed by the fledgling Jewish State. Tragically, many Arab refugees from 1948 were not offered the same opportunities by the Arab states in the region. They remain stateless to this day.

THE MAJORITY OF JEWISH REFUGEES WERE ABSORBED BY THE FLEDGLING JEWISH STATE. TRAGICALLY, MANY ARAB REFUGEES FROM 1948 WERE NOT OFFERED THE SAME OPPORTUNITIES BY THE ARAB STATES IN THE REGION. THEY REMAIN STATELESS TO THIS DAY.

Jewish refugees who went to Israel from Arab lands between May 1948 and May 1972.

Arab Middle East   Israel   Arab countries

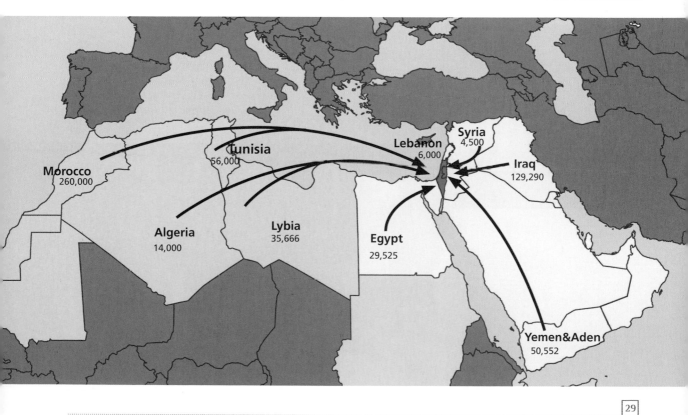

Morocco
260,000

Tunisia
56,000

Algeria
14,000

Lybia
35,666

Egypt
29,525

Lebanon
6,000

Syria
4,500

Iraq
129,290

Yemen&Aden
50,552

1967: SIX-DAY WAR

Twenty years after Israel's War of Independence, the country found itself again at war with the Arab states. This war was over in six days. Israel prevailed swiftly following a preemptive strike against Egypt, the main aggressor.

LEADUP TO THE '67 WAR

Despite the treaties and agreements of 1949, the Arab states viewed Israel as an illegitimate state and waited for their opportunity to attack again. By the late 1960s, Arab rulers believed they had gained the military advantage over their enemy. Under the leadership of President

Nasser of Egypt, they directed a series of clear provocations at Israel.

In mid-May 1967, Nasser moved two divisions of his armed forces into the Sinai Peninsula. The next day, he ordered the United Nations Emergency Force (UNEF), a peace-keeping force positioned in the Sinai, to relocate to camps in the Gaza Strip. Egypt had no authority over UNEF, but UNEF acceded to Nasser's demands.

The following week, Nasser announced a blockade against Israeli ships in the Strait of Tiran, cutting off access to and from the port city of Eilat in the south of Israel. The official declaration targeted Israel: "The Strait of Tiran is part of our territorial waters. No Israeli ship will ever navi-

Chief of Staff Lt. Gen. Yitzhak Rabin (front left) led the Israeli armed forces during the Six-Day War.

gate it again. We also forbid the shipment of strategic materials to Israel on non-Israeli vessels."

Israel appealed to the UN to break the blockade and pointed out that, under Article 51 of the UN Charter, it had the right to defend itself against an act of aggression. The UN offered no solution. Nasser, noting the sluggish international reaction, decided Israel was isolated and vulnerable.

Three days later, on May 25, the governments of Syria, Iraq, Jordan, and Saudi Arabia, following Egypt's directives, began mobilizing troops along Israel's borders. By May 31, Egypt had moved 100,000 troops, 1,000 tanks, and 500 heavy guns into the Sinai buffer zone—the area between Israel and Egypt that had been established as neutral under earlier armistice agreements.

Israel's many appeals to the UN failed to prevent a conflict. On Sunday, June 4, Israeli Prime Minister Levi Eshkol convened an emergency War Cabinet meeting and passed a resolution to launch a preemptive strike against the Arab States, now clearly poised for war. The Jewish state's 264,000 soldiers, 800 tanks, and 300 combat aircraft would attempt to defend Israel against the combined strength of the Arabs' 350,000 soldiers, 2,000 tanks, and 700 aircraft.

ARAB RHETORIC IN THE LEADUP TO THE 1967 WAR

Just before the war began, outbursts of anti-Israel statements came from Arab leaders and from the Arab states' government-controlled radios. On May 27, just a few days before the war, Nasser summed up the Arab objectives: "Our basic objective will be the destruction of Israel. The Arab people want to fight. ... The mining of Sharm el Sheikh [the Strait of Tiran] is a confrontation with Israel. Adopting this measure obligates us to be ready to embark on a general war with Israel."

Nasser's statements were followed by those of Iraqi President Aref, on May 31: "The existence of Israel is an error which must be rectified. This is our opportunity to wipe out the ignominy which has been with us since 1948. Our goal is clear—to wipe Israel off the map."

A few days later, on June 1, the chairman of the Palestine Liberation Organization (PLO), Ahmed Shukairy, declared the following: "This is a fight for a homeland. It is either us or the Israelis. There is no middle road. The Jews of Palestine will have to leave. ... Any of the old Palestine Jewish population who survive may stay, but it is my impression that none of them will survive."

ISRAEL'S MANY APPEALS TO THE UN FAILED TO PREVENT A CONFLICT. ON SUNDAY, JUNE 4, ISRAELI PRIME MINISTER LEVI ESHKOL CONVENED AN EMERGENCY WAR CABINET MEETING AND PASSED A RESOLUTION TO LAUNCH A PREEMPTIVE STRIKE AGAINST THE ARAB STATES.

Israel's decisive victory in the Six-Day War included the capture of the Gaza Strip and the Sinai Peninsula from Egypt, the West Bank and East Jerusalem from Jordan, and the Golan Heights from Syria.

MAIN EVENTS OF THE WAR

On June 5, 1967, Israel launched an aerial attack that destroyed almost all of the Egyptian air force. The Israeli prime minister sent word to King Hussein of Jordan, through the UN and the Americans, that if Jordan stayed out of the war, Israel would not attack them. Had Jordan complied, its occupation of the West Bank and the Old City of Jerusalem would have continued as it had since 1948. That did not happen, however. Jordan's response was to shell Israel.

Chief of Staff Lt. Gen. Yitzhak Rabin (left) in the entrance to the old city of Jerusalem during the Six Day War, with Moshe Dayan (center) and Uzi Narkiss.

Once Jordan joined the war, the Israeli Cabinet gave the go-ahead to the Israel Defense Forces (IDF) to take the Old City of Jerusalem. When the Israelis entered the Old City in June 1967, they found that all but one of the 35 synagogues there had been destroyed. These synagogues were centuries old. In the ancient graveyard on the Mount of Olives, the Jordanians had defaced or profaned 38,000 of the 50,000 Jewish graves. Nonetheless, recapturing the Old City was a profoundly joyful event for the Jewish people. When Israeli soldiers prayed at the Western Wall on June 7, 1967, it marked the end of nearly 2,000 years of restricted Jewish access to their holiest site—the Temple Mount.

Shortly after capturing the Temple Mount/Haram al-Sharif in the Old City, the government of Israel made the decision to return custody of it to Muslim administrators. This was a remarkable decision, considering that Jewish access to the area had been denied under Jordanian occupation and that the Temple Mount is the holiest site in Judaism.

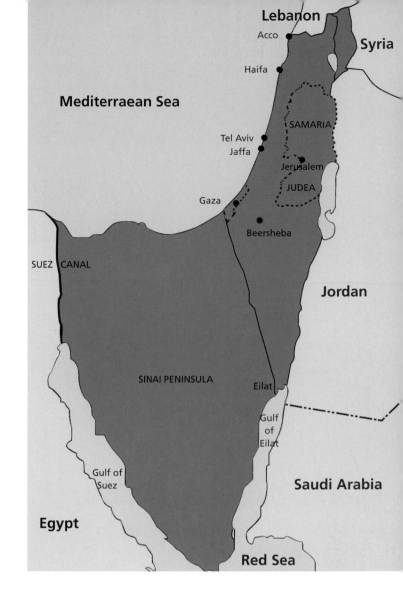

At the end of the Six-Day War, Israel controlled the West Bank, the Gaza Strip, the Sinai Peninsula, and the Golan Heights. Before the war, all of these territories had been held by the defeated Arab nations.

POLITICAL AFTERMATH OF THE 1967 WAR

Two weeks after the war, the Israeli parliament—the Knesset—enacted legislation to include the Old City and east Jerusalem under Israeli administration and Israeli law. A week later, the UN General Assembly passed Resolution 2253, declaring Israel's measures invalid and calling upon the Israeli government to rescind them. Since then, the UN has opposed Israel's reunification of Jerusalem and its claims to sovereignty over it.

Israel's new legislation also included the Protection of Holy Places Law 5727 (1967). This Act stipulated that holy places were to be protected from desecration and "anything likely to violate the freedom of access of the members of the different religions to the places sacred to them or their feelings with regard to those places." Israel gave the Muslim Waqf—the governing body that oversees Muslim endowments—the authority to administer various Muslim holy sites, including the Temple Mount/Haram Al-Sharif, the Dome of the Rock, and the Al-Aqsa Mosque. Since 1967, Israel has continued to protect all faiths' freedom of access to their holy sites.

Territory held by Israel after the 1967 War.

Arab States

Israel's Territory

SINCE 1967, ISRAEL HAS CONTINUED TO PROTECT ALL FAITHS' FREEDOM OF ACCESS TO THEIR HOLY SITES.

THE YOM KIPPUR WAR, THE OIL EMBARGO, AND THEIR EFFECTS

The Yom Kippur War began with a massive and successful Egyptian crossing of the Suez Canal.

On Saturday October 6, 1973, while Israel was engaged in the holy day services of Yom Kippur and the Jewish Sabbath, Egypt and Syria launched a surprise attack on the country's southern front, near the Suez Canal, and on the northern front of the Golan Heights. Many Israeli soldiers on those fronts were not at their usual positions because of the holy day. The first days of the war were dire for the Israelis. By the fifth day, however, Israel had managed to regroup, and the tide turned against the Arab forces. The war ended with a cease-fire on October 24, 1973.

The Arab defeat led to a change in their strategy of aggression toward Israel.

They continued to wage war, but now it was a non-military war. In 1973, members of the Organization of Arab Petroleum Exporting Countries (OAPEC) declared an oil embargo. The "oil weapon" targeted not just the US, but also the industrialized nations of Great Britain, Canada, Japan, and the Netherlands. The Arab states' hope was that the embargo would change these governments' foreign policies towards Israel. The resulting "oil crisis," which started in October 1973, lasted until March 1974.

The strategy was successful. Western Europe and Japan began changing their Middle East policies. For example, Great Britain began refusing to allow the United States to use British bases to airlift supplies to Israel.

The non-military war marked the beginning of a propaganda war on Israel waged by the Arab States.

The first days of the war were dire for the Israelis. By the fifth day, however, Israel had managed to regroup, and the tide turned against the Arab forces.

ENDORSEMENT OF THE PLO

Following the OAPEC oil embargo, there was a crucial meeting of the League of Arab States in Rabat, Morocco, in October 1974. The Rabat Summit brought together the representatives of the PLO and the leaders of 20 Arab states. The Rabat Summit marked the first time that all of the Arab states officially recognized the PLO as the "sole legitimate representative of the 'Palestinian' people." The Arab states also gave official recognition to the PLO's territorial claims to the West Bank.

Following the Rabat Summit, the UN General Assembly took measures that essentially aligned it with the Arab states. First, it made the decision to grant the PLO "Permanent Observer" status. Giving a non-state actor like the PLO such international legitimacy was unprecedented. The UN also established a new permanent committee under the name "Committee on the Exercise of the Inalienable Rights of the Palestinian People." This committee's main task was to make recommendations that would lead to the realization of Palestinian political rights. These rights were now officially recognized by the UN. From this point on, the number of the UN Resolutions targeting Israel increased dramatically, and their tone became more hostile.

UN CONDEMNATION OF ISRAEL

On November 10, 1975, the UN General Assembly adopted Resolution 3379. This resolution de-

clared Zionism to be a form of "racism and racial discrimination." It denounced Israel as the "racist regime in occupied Palestine" whose policies were aimed "at repression of the dignity and integrity of the human being." It associated Israel and Zionism with South African apartheid, colonialism, occupation, and imperialism. This resolution was later revoked by the UN. However, it left a legacy damaging to Israel. For example, there are now annual demonstrations against Israel on university campuses in the US, during what students call "Israel Apartheid Week."

Following the 1973 war and the Arab oil embargo, Israel became the target of more UN sanctions than any other country. Between 1948 and 1982, the UN "condemned," "deplored," or "censured" Israel 38 times. The Arab states were not sanctioned at all. While some approved of this trend, others were troubled by it and saw it as grounds for doubting the UN's neutrality. As one jurist remarked, "Unless one believes that the Israeli–Arab dispute is essentially one between demons and angels, this figure is cause for some concern."

Industrial countries were severely disadvantaged when OAPEC executives declared the oil embargo in 1973. The price of oil quadrupled by 1974 and a gas rationing system had to be introduced in many places.

ISRAEL: 1987 TO THE PRESENT

From 1987 to the present, the socio-political context of Israel and the Palestinians has featured two closely related dynamics. There have been uprisings, terrorism, and war; and there have been peace proposals.

THE INTIFADA AND ITS AFTERMATH (1987)

On December 9, 1987, a grassroots Palestinian uprising known as the *intifada* (the Arabic term for "shaking off " or "uprising") began in Gaza and spread through the Arab towns and villages of the West Bank (Judea and Samaria). It was intended to pressure Israel and to attract international support for an independent Palestinian state. During the next three years, terrorist attacks killed dozens of Jewish soldiers and civilians. These attacks led, by way of Israeli retaliation, to hundreds of Arab deaths. Injuries on both sides were in the thousands.

A number of factors gave rise to the intifada. One was the perception among Palestinian Arabs, especially the young, that they couldn't count on either the Arab states, Israel, the international community, or their own leadership to resolve their problems.

Yitzhak Rabin, the Israeli minister of defence, tried to crush the rebellion with a harsh iron-fist policy. Israeli forces used rubber bullets and tear gas against demonstrators, imposed curfews, and imprisoned thousands of Palestinian Arabs, including leading activists. These tough measures earned Israel international disapproval as well as domestic stress. By 1987, the world media was portraying Israel as a harsh oppressor, and the Palestinian Arabs as the oppressed.

For the past three decades, the world media has portrayed Israel as a harsh oppressor, and the Palestinian Arabs as the oppressed.

FORMATION OF HAMAS

As the intifada continued, Yasser Arafat's PLO began losing ground in Gaza to a young, fast-growing political faction known as *Hamas* (Arabic for "enthusiasm" or "zeal"). Hamas is an Egyptian-based Muslim Brotherhood movement whose aim is to establish an Islamist Palestinian society. The ideology of Hamas is much more extreme than the secular ideology of Fatah, the dominant faction within the PLO.

PLO ANNOUNCEMENT OF PALESTINIAN STATE (1988)

Conscious of losing support to Hamas among the Palestinian people of Gaza, Arafat announced in 1988 a plan for a two-state solution, with Jerusalem as the Palestinian capital. He included the West Bank and Gaza in his planned Palestinian state. On December 14, he spoke to the UN General Assembly, claiming that the establishment of the State of Palestine is based on the Palestinian Arab people's natural, historic, and legal right to their homeland.

Arafat's contention that the Arabs were entitled to self-determination and sovereignty rights in Palestine according to international law was not—as we have seen—actually in keeping with legal precedent. As previously discussed, the Mandate for Palestine guaranteed the Arab inhabitants of Palestine their civil and religious rights in Palestine, but not political rights of self-determination and sovereignty. Those rights were reserved for the region's prospective Jewish inhabitants.

HAMAS CHARTER

The Hamas Charter includes the following provisions:

Article 11: The Islamic Resistance Movement believes that the land of Palestine is an Islamic Waqf consecrated for future Moslem generations until Judgement Day. It, or any part of it, should not be squandered: it, or any part of it, should not be given up. ...

Article 13: Initiatives, and so-called peaceful solutions and international conferences, are in contradiction to the principles of the Islamic Resistance Movement. ... There is no solution for the Palestinian question except through Jihad [Holy War].

Article 15: It is necessary to instill in the minds of the Moslem generations that the Palestinian problem is a religious problem, and should be dealt with on this basis.

JORDAN'S RESPONSE TO THE INTIFADA

The intifada, as well as having a dismal effect on the economies and daily lives in the disputed territories, intensified the Palestinian refugee problem. It pushed Jordan to sever ties with the Palestinian Arabs.

After the 1948 war, the government of Jordan had extended full Jordanian citizenship to Palestinian Arabs who had taken refuge in Jordan or who had remained in areas of the West Bank controlled by Jordan. (It was the only Arab state to acknowledge the Palestinians in this way.) In the early 1980s, Jordan began to change these citizenship policies. In the intifada's wake, King Hussein of Jordan announced that Jordan was relinquishing its claims to sovereignty over the West Bank and terminating its ties with the Palestinian Arabs living there. Hussein's severing these ties meant revoking their Jordanian citizenship status. Overnight, over 1 million Palestinian Arabs became stateless.

Police and security personnel inspecting the remains of a burnt-out public transportation bus in Haifa during the intifada. The attacks by militant wings of Fatah and Hamas claimed the lives of 305 men, women, and children, and left hundreds of others maimed or injured.

US President George W. Bush (center), Israeli Prime Minister Ariel Sharon (right) and Palestinian Prime Minister Mahmoud Abbas (left) during the Red Sea Summit in Jordan, in 2003. The purpose of the summit was to boost President Bush's Roadmap for Peace. Despite the pledges of both sides, there was little progress in implementing the Roadmap, as violence continued.

THE AL-AQSA INTIFADA (2000)

Amid the tensions caused by the failed talks at Camp David, Ariel Sharon, then leader of the opposition in Israel, visited the Temple Mount on September 28, 2000. He was accompanied by a small group of Israelis and a large contingent of Israeli police. This visit triggered severe violence and riots throughout the West Bank, the Gaza Strip, and within the Arab communities inside Israel. The Palestinians blamed Sharon's visit for the uprising, which is often referred to as the "Al-Aqsa Intifada." The Israelis, in turn, blamed Arafat, saying that the intifada was planned long before the Temple Mount visit and that it was Arafat's way of deflecting the negative attention he'd received over Camp David.

Despite the escalating violence, peace initiatives continued for the next four years. There were negotiations in January 2001, on the eve of the Israeli elections, in Taba on the Sinai Peninsula. These were followed, in 2002, by another attempt to solve the Israeli–Palestinian conflict—namely, the "Road Map" or Performance-Based Proposal. This came about through the initiatives of the United States, the European Union, Russia, and the UN (collectively referred to as the "Quartet"). This plan involved several phases, and it resembled previous initiatives in the following respects:

- It was based on the principle of land for peace;

- Territorial boundaries would be based on UN resolutions 242 and 338;

- It required of the PA full recognition of Israel;

- It granted Israelis the right to live in peace and security; and

- It required Israel to freeze settlement building in the West Bank.

The peace efforts continued, but so did the violence. The number of suicide bombings in Israel increased from four in 2000 to a peak of 55 in 2002.

THE SECURITY BARRIER (2002)

The attacks by militant wings of Fatah and Hamas claimed the lives of 305 men, women, and children, and left hundreds of others maimed or injured. In 2002, the Israeli government decided to build a security barrier to protect their citizens from the suicide bombings. The barrier became the focus of much negative international attention. Its success in preventing attacks was undeniable, however. As its construction progressed, the number of attacks and casualties dropped by approximately 50 percent each year until, in 2007, there was only one attack.

The security barrier was built by Israel along the 1949 Armistice Line ("Green Line"). The barrier protects civilians from Palestinian terrorism, especially suicide bombing attacks.

HOT TOPIC
IS THE SECURITY BARRIER JUSTIFIED?

Because the barrier was successful in its practical aims, the majority of Israelis supported its construction. On the other hand, Israelis and Palestinians living on the east side of the barrier were vehemently opposed to it; the barrier interfered with their freedom of movement and their access to services and land.

The UN did not view the barrier as justified and asked the International Court of Justice (ICJ) to rule on its legality. On July 9, 2004, the ICJ issued the following statement: "The Court finds that the construction by Israel of a wall in the Occupied Palestinian Territory and its associated régime are contrary to international law."

The ICJ's opinion stated that the territory upon which the security barrier was built belonged to the Palestinians. International jurist Dr. Jacques Gauthier noted that the ICJ opinion, by failing to consider the earlier legal decisions regarding Palestine (under the Mandate for Palestine, for example) "takes away the rights and entitlements acquired by the Jewish people over the last century."

The ICJ ruling on the security barrier also did not take into consideration Israel's right as a member state of the United Nations to take measures to protect its civilian population, which, in 2002, included not just Jews but over 1 million Arabs.

The graph below shows the effectivness of the barrier in preventing terrorist attacks. As its construction progressed, the number of attacks and casualties dropped by approximately 50 percent each year.

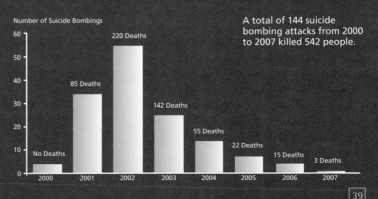

Number of Suicide Bombings

A total of 144 suicide bombing attacks from 2000 to 2007 killed 542 people.

CONCLUSION

The land of Israel has figured large in human consciousness since the beginning of civilized life on earth. To the great empires of the ancient past—Egypt, Assyria, and Babylon—it was a place of strategic importance, a juncture for trade and a springboard for imperial conquest and control. In time it became the cherished homeland, divinely promised and in time possessed, of the Israelites. Their story, told in the Bible and essential to three of the world's great religions, has shaped the spiritual course of the world. The jewel of this land is Jerusalem, site of the Temple Mount, of the Church of the Holy Sepulchre, and of the Dome of the Rock. In European maps of five hundred years ago, Jerusalem was shown as the hub of the world.

All the maps have been redrawn since then. Old empires have vanished, new ones rising in their stead. And yet Israel, that narrow strip of land, still lays an insistent claim to the world's regard. It remains central, sacred to half the peoples of the world, still the subject of strong territorial passions. It is contested no less fiercely today than it was in past millennia, by Israelites and Philistines, by Babylonians and Persians, by Islamic caliphates and European crusaders. Now as then, its affairs and its destiny preoccupy us.

The Jewish people who now possess the land have an ancient claim to it. Their modern title to Israel, though challenged and deplored in some quarters, is rooted in history and justified by international law. However, from the moment it was ceded to them, the Israelis have had to defend this right of ownership continually, by argument and by military force. Their struggle is ongoing. The main opponent is another ancient Semitic people, the Arabs, who have a long history in the region and a determined wish to make the land their own.

The Arab states, having started the wars that displaced the Palestinian Arabs from their homes in 1948, have kept them in camps for over 60 years, refusing them citizenship in their own lands. Many in the international community view the Palestinian Arabs with sympathy, and some sympathy is justified. Neither their leaders nor their Arab brothers have served this people well. On this point, many in the international community and the media are silent. They support the Arab regimes, blaming Israel alone for the region's problems and for the

Jerusalem's hills and valleys have been central to the 4,000 year old story that continues to this day.

Palestinian Arabs' plight. The facts of history do not corroborate this blame.

History tells us that, a century ago, the entire Middle East was Ottoman territory. The Allied Powers, having seized this territory from the defeated Turks at the end of World War I, bestowed most of it on the Arabs. This gave them statehood in virtually all of the Middle East. What they weren't given was Israel, the small portion of land the Allied Powers set aside as a prospective state for the Jewish people. The Arabs accepted those of the Allied Powers' decisions that were to their benefit, but refused any benefit to Israel. Their refusal, in the form of violent opposition, continues to this day.

As a result, Israel faces major challenges today. The international community regards the two-state solution, with borders based on the 1949 Armistice Line and Jerusalem divided, as the only way of ending the Arab–Israeli impasse. This solution poses an enormous security risk for Israel. The international pressure to accept it is among Israel's contemporary challenges, as is the pressure to absorb millions of potentially hostile Arab refugees, descendants of those dislodged from Israel by the 1948 war. Another challenge facing Israel today stems from its being the only democratic state in a region increasingly overrun by authoritarian, anti-democratic ideologies.

The discourse surrounding the modern State of Israel is too often shaped by partisan passions and by facile, simplified perspectives. A person who wishes to avoid these traps must carefully sift the grounds, historical, religious, and legal, of the Arab and the Israeli claims to the land. Critical thinking is crucial, and so is knowledge. A clear-eyed consideration of its long and intricate history, from ancient roots to the present day, is the key to grasping the challenges that confront Israel and the region. And it is the key to appraising the possible solutions.

CRITICAL THINKING IS CRUCIAL, AND SO IS KNOWLEDGE. A CLEAR-EYED CONSIDERATION OF ISRAEL'S LONG AND INTRICATE HISTORY IS THE KEY TO GRASPING THE CHALLENGES THAT CONFRONT THIS REGION.

REFERENCES

Page 7:   [El Amarna Letters] H.H. Ben Sasson, ed., *A History of the Jewish People*, (Cambridge: Harvard University Press, 1976), 9.

Page 9:   [quotation re protohistory] H.H. Ben Sasson, ed., *A History of the Jewish People*, (Cambridge: Harvard University Press, 1976), 28.

Page 18:   [excerpt from the McMahon–Hussein correspondence] George Antonius, *The Arab Awakening* (Safety Harbor, Fl: Simon Publications, 2001), 419.

Page 18:   [McMahon quotation] "Report of a Committee Set up to Consider Certain Correspondence Between Sir Henry McMahon and he Sharif of Mecca in 1915 and 1916, Secretary of State for the Colonies," (London: March 16, 1939), accessed March 18, 2012, http://unispal.un.org/UNISPAL.NSF/0/4C4F7515DC39195185256CF7006F878C. *Note:* George Antonius was among the representatives of the Arab Delegation at these meetings.

Page 23:   [cradle and home of their vital race] David Hunter Miller, "Document 246: Outline of Tentative Report and Recommendation Prepared by the Intelligence Section, In Accordance with Instructions for the President and the Plenipotentiaries, January 21,1919," in *My Diary at the Conference of Paris: With Documents* (NewYork, 1924), 4: 264. *Note:* David Hunter Miller was a member of the U.S. delegation at the Peace Conference and compiled a 21-volume diary.

Page 30–31:   [Nasser on the Strait of Tiran] Quoted in Jacques Paul Gauthier, *Sovereignty Over the Old City of Jerusalem: A Study of the Historical, Religious, Political and Legal Aspects of the Question of the Old City*, Thèse No. 725 (Geneva: Université de Genève, 2007), 670.

Page 31:   [Arab rhetoric] Quoted in Martin Gilbert, *The Routledge Atlas of the Arab-Israeli Conflict*, 9th ed. (London: Routledge, 2008), 66–67.

Page 33:   [legislation] State of Israel, *Protection of Holy Places Law* 5727, June 27, 1967, http://www.knesset.gov.il/ laws/special/eng/HolyPlaces.htm.

Page 35:   [on UN neutrality] Ilan Dunsky. "Israel, the Arabs and International Law: Whose Palestine Is It, Anyway?" *Dalhousie Journal of Legal Studies* 2 (1993)

Page 39:   [ICJ opinion on the security barrier] International Court of Justice,"Legal Consequences of the Construction of a Wall in the Occupied Palestinian Territory," Press Release 2004/28, July 9, 2004, http://www.icj-cij.org/docket/index.php ?pr=71&code=m-wp&tp1=3&tp2=4&tp3=6&ca.

Page 39:   [rights and entitlements] Jacques Paul Gauthier, *Sovereignty Over the Old City of Jerusalem: A Study of the Historical, Religious, Political and Legal Aspects of the Question of the Old City*, Thèse No. 725 (Geneva: Université de Genève, 2007), 781.

CHRISTIANS UNITED FOR ISRAEL

"I consider CUFI to be a vital part of Israel's national security."
Prime Minister Netanyahu

"CUFI is America's largest and most dependable pro-Israel group."
The Washington Post

"Christians United for Israel jumps to the forefront of pro-Israel groups."
The Hill

"I do not know of an organization in the world more important to Israel than CUFI."
Dr. Charles Krauthammer

As the world grows increasingly dangerous, Israel has become an even more significant force for moral clarity and strength. And in order to protect her in the United States, Christians United for Israel (CUFI) has enlisted a massive advocacy army.

CUFI is the largest pro-Israel organization in the U.S., with over 3 million members and 1.2 million Facebook fans. We educate America's Christians about the biblical and moral imperative to support Israel. We equip America's Christians to defend Israel in their churches, communities, online and in our nation's capital.

We're also investing to win the long-term battle for the hearts and minds of the rising generation so that Christian support for Israel will survive for generations to come. Through our student program, *CUFI On Campus*, CUFI is changing the Israel conversation on college campuses. *CUFI on Campus* develops biblically and politically minded student leaders and equips them to become effective advocates for Israel on their college campuses. CUFI is transforming Millennial Christian leaders' views on Israel through the Israel Collective, which resuscitates the fading millennial Christian generation's support for Israel by educating the most influential millennial Christians in America.

We utilize traditional and new media to reach millions of Americans with pro-Israel messages. We have published full page ads in major newspapers across the country, placed billboards in highly trafficked areas, produced a full length film, and utilized our eight social media channels to reach millions of people world wide.

Our impact has been IMMEDIATE.
Our growth has been REMARKABLE.
And we've only JUST BEGUN.

ABOUT THE AUTHOR

RICHARD BASS is the author of *Israel in World Relations* and creator of the *For Critical Thinkers* YouTube video series and books, which have become some of the most sought after contemporary resources for education concerning Israel. A career educator in the subjects of law and philosophy, Richard emphasizes critical thinking in his works—the process of analyzing claims, uncovering facts, and evaluating arguments, especially in connection with controversial topics and crucial issues. A former Purdue University football coach and golf professional, Richard has given presentations on Israel to diverse audiences around the world, including senators and members of Parliament, professional educators, Jewish and Christian communities, and university student groups.